# Preparing for Eternity

# Preparing for Eternity

## Alexander Nisbet

REFORMATION PRESS
2019

British Library Cataloguing in Publication Data
ISBN 978-1-912042-06-7

© Reformation Press 2019

Originally published in 1694 as part of
*An Exposition with Practical Observations Upon the
Book of Ecclesiastes*
Edited and annotated by R. J. Dickie and M. Vogan

Published by Reformation Press
11 Churchill Drive, Stornoway
Isle of Lewis, Scotland HS1 2NP
www.reformationpress.co.uk

Printed by www.lulu.com

Also available as a Kindle e-book
ISBN 978-1-912042-07-4

All rights reserved. No part of this publication may be reproduced, stored in a retrieval system, or transmitted, in any form or by any means, without the prior permission in writing of Reformation Press, or as expressly permitted by law, by licence, or under terms agreed with the appropriate reprographic rights organisation.

# Contents

| | |
|---|---|
| Introduction | 7 |
| An overview of Ecclesiastes chapter 12 | 11 |
| Verse 1 Making preparation | 18 |
| Verse 2 Declining comforts | 25 |
| Verse 3 A besieged castle | 30 |
| Verse 4 Declining strength | 35 |
| Verse 5 Increasing fears | 40 |
| Verse 6 Physical weakening | 46 |
| Verse 7 Beyond death | 52 |
| Verse 8 A considered verdict | 56 |
| Verse 9 The diligent preacher | 60 |
| Verse 10 Acceptable words | 67 |
| Verse 11 Wise words | 71 |
| Verse 12 Profitable study | 76 |
| Verse 13 Fear God | 81 |
| Verse 14 The Final Judgment | 86 |

# Introduction

WE must prepare for eternity and we cannot put it off until we think it is imminent. We cannot guarantee that we will have the ability to do this in the time of sickness or old age. Ecclesiastes chapter 12 urges this wise instruction through striking pictures of physical decline. Alexander Nisbet draws out the way in which this spiritual wisdom applies urgently to each one of us.

Alexander Nisbet of Knock (1623–69) was a Covenanting minister who was one of the landed nobility.[1] He graduated from Edinburgh University in 1643 and was ordained to the Second Charge of Irvine, Ayrshire, around 1646. He moved to the First Charge in 1650, and was ejected in 1662 when Episcopacy was re-established.[2] Nisbet died on 11 March 1669, aged 46.[3]

One of his fellow ministers wrote a Latin epitaph, *Grande aliquid vultu nituit, gressuque decoro; grandius in magni*

---

[1] The lands of Knock were in the Cunninghame district of Ayrshire. A charter was granted in relation to these lands of Knock in the year before he died.

[2] Hew Scott, ed., *Fasti Ecclesiae Scoticanae: The Succession of Ministers in the Church of Scotland from the Reformation*, Vol. 3: Synod of Glasgow and Ayr (Edinburgh: Oliver and Boyd, 1920), p. 99.

[3] Robert Wodrow says Nisbet died in 1668. Robert Wodrow, *Analecta or Materials for a History of Remarkable Providences*, 4 vols., (Edinburgh: Maitland Club, 1842–3), Vol. 1, p. 168.

*dotibus ingenui*,[4] which may be rendered in English as: Something grand shone in both his countenance and handsome step; grander still amidst the endowments of a great noble.

The last years of Nisbet's life appear to have been occupied with completing the exposition of Ecclesiastes and preparing it for publication. Through the efforts of Patrick Warner it was finally published in 1694 after the persecution ended. Warner was Nisbet's successor as minister of Irvine.[5,6] As Warner notes in the preface to the original book, the exposition benefits from a period when Nisbet 'had taken a

---

[4] *The New Statistical Account of Scotland: Ayr, Bute*, (Edinburgh: William Blackwood, 1845), Vol. 5, p. 630.

[5] The book was not published until 1694, six years after the persecution ended and nine years after Charles II's death. This was because of certain comments on obedience to civil government in relation to 'the word of a king' in Ecclesiastes 8:4. Nisbet's remarks were not favourable to the absolute monarchy claimed by Charles II and so the book was not submitted for publication earlier as such comments would have been prosecuted as treason.

[6] Patrick Warner of Ardeer was born in Irvine in 1640. He was ordained in London in 1669. He went to India and officiated at Fort St George, on the Coromandel coast, for three years. He returned in 1677 and preached occasionally. After the battle of Bothwell Bridge in 1679, he went to Holland, where he remained till 1681. Having returned to Scotland, he was arrested in Feb. 1682, and imprisoned in Edinburgh on 7th June, but was released on undertaking to leave the kingdom. He then went to Tweedmouth and Newcastle, but was again imprisoned for eight weeks for not taking the Oath of Allegiance. When released he went to Rotterdam and returned in 1687. He ministered in Irvine from 1688. He resigned his charge, 28 July 1702, apparently through discouragements. Hew Scott, *Fasti Ecclesiae Scoticanae*, Vol. 3, pp. 99–100; *The New Statistical Account of Scotland* (see above).

# Introduction

review of his bypast life; as he was indeed a very serious observer both of his own life, and of the passages of God's providence about him, yea and a recorder of both'. It helped him to be weaned to a greater extent 'from the world and all its vain pleasures and delights'. He attained to this 'in a great measure'. It fitted and prepared him in a notable way 'for his great change, and made his passage from this life to a better, sweet, easy and comfortable'.

Warner informs us of Nisbet's 'rare skill in the original languages, especially in the Hebrew, wherein he greatly excelled'. The exposition is not, however, intended to be a learned commentary. Like the commentaries of David Dickson, George Hutcheson and James Fergusson, it follows a distinctive approach not found in other authors. There is brief and succinct explanation of a verse. This is followed by a comprehensive set of practical observations and application. The intended readership consisted of ordinary people rather than ministers or scholars.

In publishing Nisbet's exposition of Ecclesiastes, Patrick Warner commends his 'great judgment and singular dexterity in opening and expounding the Scripture'. Nisbet also published a highly regarded Exposition of 1 & 2 Peter in 1658.[7] Little is known of his life and he seems to have been especially modest. He offered his exposition of 1 & 2 Peter to help someone else produce a commentary but David Dickson and George Hutcheson esteemed Nisbet's work so highly that they arranged for it to be published.

---

[7] Currently published by the Banner of Truth Trust as one of the *Geneva Series of Commentaries*.

Warner shows why Nisbet's exposition is so helpful for us. If you 'would gladly have your heart weaned from the world, rise above its vain pleasures and have your life in heaven, as a stranger and pilgrim on this earth … this will influence you to carefully peruse this piece [book], and look to the Lord for his blessing with it, that it may have this effect on you.'[8]

Matthew Vogan<br>
Carrington, Midlothian

---

[8] In preparing the present volume for publication, the text has been edited to modernise spelling, archaic grammatical constructions, punctuation and layout. Unduly long sentences have been split into shorter sentences with minor adjustments of wording to accommodate the changes. The English meanings of Scots words have been included in brackets or as footnotes, based on the *Dictionary of the Scots Language* (www.dsl.ac.uk). The *Oxford English Dictionary* has been the basis for similar renderings of obscure, archaic, or ambiguous English words. The aim has been to make the text accessible to modern readers whilst being faithful to the original text.

# An overview of Ecclesiastes chapter 12

## The first part of the chapter—verses 1 to 7

IN the first part of this chapter contained to the seventh verse, the Preacher continues his purpose [intention] begun in the end of the last chapter, which is to stir up men [people] to a serious and timeous [early] preparation for death and judgment.

1. And in order to do this he presses [urges] the exercise of a duty very fit and necessary for that end, to remember their Creator in the days of their youth (verse 1). In it we have:

> 1) The duty itself, which is to remember, a word importing [signifying] a clear up-taking [understanding] of God and his attributes, an affectionate and cordial trusting in him, and an engagement to the duties of new obedience (verse 1).
> 2) The season fittest [most suitable] for discharge of that duty, not only the present now, but the time of youth (verse 1).
> 3) The argument by which he presses this duty, taken from the sad condition that every man [person] is to expect under old age, with reference to the trouble

and afflictions incident to it, and the continuance of these afflictions upon him, and the language that such will have at such a time, far different from what they had in their youth (verse 1).

2. He negatively describes the fittest opportunities for the performance of these duties necessary, in order to prepare for death, as that it should not be deferred till the miseries of old age creep on, nor till the frequent returns of outward afflictions, especially diseases (verse 2).

In the dimness of the bodily eyes, the usefulness of external lights and the failing of the reason, held forth by the allegories of the sun, moon and stars being darkened, and in the continual succession (as one cloud or shower after another comes in time of winter) of one trouble after another (verse 2).

3. The Preacher positively evinces [proves] the time of old age not to be so fit an opportunity for making peace with God in order to preparation for death as the time of youth and health, an old man's body being so beset with death (as a besieged castle) that the arms and hands (called the keepers of the house) do shake, the legs and thighs (the strong men) grow feeble, the teeth (the grinders) turn few, loose and unfit for preparing meat for the stomach, and the eyes (which took out at their holes as windows) grow dim and weak (verse 3).

4. By several other metaphors he describes the dissolution of this house of clay, or earthly tabernacle, as:

An Overview of Ecclesiastes Chapter 12

1) By the shutting of the doors in the street (importing the unfitness of the mouth and lips to speak, or throat, which are the doors of the tabernacle to let down meat), by the low sounding of the grinders (holding out the small noise old men, through want [lack] or weakness of their teeth, make in their eating), by his rising at the voice of the bird (thereby signifying the unsoundness of his sleep), and by the daughters of music brought low (thereby discovering [revealing] the weakness of all these organs of the body made use of either in uttering or receiving of melodious sounds) (verse 4).

2) By old and dying men being afraid of that which is high, and their fears in the way (insinuating their want of strength and courage), by the flourishing of the almond tree (holding forth the increase of grey hairs as a forerunner of death), by the grasshoppers being a burden, showing their weakness to be such, as that the weight of a fly shall be a trouble to them. And by the failing of the desire, both after lawful and unlawful objects. The ground of all of which is because man is going to his unchangeable estate, and his friends have given him over for dead and begun their mourning for him (verse 5).

3) By the loosing of the silver cord, holding forth the decay of the natural life and spirits, or marrow of the backbone [spinal cord] and arteries of the heart, which thence convoy [conduct] the spirits to other

places of the body.⁹ By the breaking of the golden bowl, whereby is meant the skin containing the brain [the *dura mater*] which, having the pores of it much opened to admit [allow in] what is prejudicial,¹⁰ foretokens [signals] a decay of the body in old age.

4) By the breaking of the pitcher at the fountain, by which is meant the obstruction of a vein, in the form of a pitcher coming from the liver (here called the fountain) betokening [denoting] decay and death (verse 6).

5) And by the wheel broken at the cistern, by which is meant the lungs, which as a wheel are in continual motion, till by watery humours [fluids] and phlegm¹¹ falling down in the stomach, they be impeded, and so it brings decay and death (verse 6).

All of this drives the Preacher's scope in verse 1 to prepare for death in time before these things fall out, by remembering their Creator in the days of youth.

5. And this first part of the chapter is shut up [concluded] in giving a short sum (the tabernacle being dissolved, as is

---

⁹ In Nisbet's time it was believed that 'the spirits' were a highly refined fluid which permeated and gave life to the blood and chief organs of the body.

¹⁰ A further mistaken health belief in Nisbet's days.

¹¹ Until the Late Middle Ages, the metaphysical theories of the second century physician, Galen, prevailed. He taught that there were four humours or fluids which determined a person's physical and mental qualities—blood, phlegm, choler and melancholy. It is not uncommon to find references to these theories long after they had been overtaken by advances in medical knowledge.

before described) of man's future state, both as to the body, that it being dust in its first original, returns to that till the resurrection, and also as to the soul, here called the spirit, because of its immaterial substance and resemblance to God, that it shall return to God to be disposed of eternally by him. This also may persuade to the duty of preparing for death (verse 7).

## The second part of the chapter—verses 8 to 14

In the second part of this chapter, from verse 8 to the end, the Preacher sums up this purpose and the whole book, in which:

1. He asserts (as the substance of this book) the vanity and insufficiency of all human things for directing man to true happiness (verse 8).

2. He commends the purpose contained in this book:

> 1) From the Preacher himself and his qualification of wisdom as from the improvement [spiritual benefit] he made of this for the good of the Church, as from his diligence and assiduity in his work, as from his not resting in any measure attained, but seeking out carefully for more, as from his watchfulness and giving good heed, as from his orderly digesting of his matter, so from his dexterity in reducing purposes to short and grave sentences or proverbs (verse 9).

2) From the qualities of the doctrine delivered by him, namely, the desirableness of the words and matter, the approvableness [approvable quality] and uprightness of the purpose, and the firmness and truth of it (verse 10), all of which commend his doctrine as being desirable to move the affection, upright to reform and direct the practice, and true to inform the judgment and persuade belief.

3. He commends the purpose of this book:

1) From the efficacy of it, with reference not only to the doctrine revealed in this book, but to all Truth in general, as being powerful to excite (as a goad) people to their duty and to establish and fix men (as nails) in the ways of God (verse 11).
2) From the authority of it, as being given by and derived from Christ Jesus, the one Shepherd (verse 11).
3) In the conclusion of this book and purpose, he exhorts to the right improvement of it, and the purposes in it (verse 12). In which:
   a. He gives his readers a loving compellation [title] of a son, thereby to insinuate upon [attract] their affections (verse 12).
   b. He shows the right use of these words and purposes, even to be admonished by them (verse 12).
   c. He presses this by two reasons. The first is, that if men follow not these directions, they will be endless and fruitless (as in writing many books) in their enquiries after other things and ways.

And the second reason is from the sad effect, even to the flesh, of these vain imaginations and enquiries (verse 11).

d. In this conclusion of the book he gives the scope of all this doctrine delivered (verse 13), which:

(i) He presses on his own heart and the hearts of others (verse 13).

(ii) He branches out the substance of his whole doctrine in two duties. The first is the fear of God. The second is the keeping of his commandments (verse 13).

(iii) He presses these duties by two arguments, the first of which is in this verse 13 as being the short sum of all that God requires of and works in man, and wherewith they should be wholly employed (verse 13). The second reason by which the study of those great duties is pressed is taken from the certainty, terribleness and exactness of the Last Judgment, contained in verse last [the final verse]. And therefore, whoever design [intend] to be truly happy should forbear following lying vanities within time and give themselves to the study and exercise of fearing God and keeping his commandments, in which true preparation for death and eternity consists.

# 1

# Making preparation

Verse 1

*Remember now thy Creator in the days of thy youth, while the evil days come not, nor the years draw nigh, when thou shalt say, I have no pleasure in them.*

THE scope of this heavenly Preacher in the first part of this chapter is to stir up men to make timeous preparation for death and judgment.

1. And so in this verse he first presses that exercise which mainly fits men for appearing before their Judge in these words: 'Remember thy Creator.' According to the frequent use of the word in Scripture, it is meant that men should labour to entertain such clear thoughts of the properties of God, particularly his power and terror (Nehemiah 4:14), his grace and love (Song 1:4), as use to be [as are usually] blessed for leading men to repentance (Psalm 22:27), drawing their hearts to trust in the Lord (Psalm 20:7) and engaging them

## VERSE 1—MAKING PREPARATION

to his praise (Psalm 97:12) and to all duties of new obedience (Deuteronomy 8:11).

And while he presses this exercise on men, he represents the Lord to them as Creator, not to exclude other considerations of him as useful to be remembered by them, but because under this consideration he is naturally known to men. And this is very effectual for moving them to live to him from whom they have their being, and constantly to depend upon him from whom they have their daily preservation, which is to them a continued creation.[12]

2. Next, he points out the fittest season for the discharge of this duty, and that is the present now, and especially the days of youth, not as if these who have never gone about this duty till youth be past were not here spoken to, but because the time of youth is of all others the fittest for that exercise.

3. And thirdly, he presses us to make use of this opportunity now by a reason (which is much enlarged in the following words) taken from the sad times which every man may expect under sickness and old age. And this he sets forth in two expressions. The one is 'while the evil days come not', by which he means the days of affliction which are called by that name elsewhere in Scripture (Psalm 49:5). The other is 'and the years wherein thou shalt say, I have no pleasure in

---

[12] Protestant theologians speak of the conservation of created things as continued creation because all things would revert to nothing if they were not upheld by the word of God's power. It is the continuation of the creative act. This work is therefore seen as virtually equivalent to producing things out of nothing. It does not mean re-creation or any kind of pantheism.

them', by which is meant the time of the long continuance of trouble, which every man should prepare for toward the evening of his life, in which neither sinful pleasures nor the most lawful earthly delight shall be sweet to men, but they shall be forced to express (as they shall be able) their loathing of them. And therefore, seeing all men ought to expect such a time as this before them, it is every man's wisdom to study that which may yield true pleasure and comfort to his heart in the worst times that can come—and that is only God's favour and fellowship, which are to be found in the way of his fear and obedience, afterward recommended.

Hence learn:

1. It is not the naked contemplation or bare notions of God and his properties that will prepare men rightly for death or yield them true comfort at that time, but it is the heart-affecting and practical meditation of him, by which men cherish such thoughts of him as draw forth their affections upon him and make them frame their walk to his honour—for that is the force of the original word, both according to the propriety of the original language and the use of it in Scripture as was cleared [explained] in the exposition. 'Remember thy Creator.'

2. Though there is no consideration of God, under which the Scripture holds him out, which is not useful and profitable for us, yet these of his sovereignty and omnipotence (which the relation of a Creator offers to reasonable creatures) should be most frequently cherished, especially by men who have strong passions and lusts to be mortified [subdued], and great discouragements to grapple with in the

## Verse 1—Making preparation

way of their duty, that so they may take him up [view him] as one able easily to subdue these lusts and make a new creation upon their souls. Or if they continue voluntary slaves to them, he is able to destroy them, being their Creator. And if they give themselves up to his obedience, he is able to bear them through all difficulties (1 Peter 4:19) and to create peace and comfort in their spirits to make up the loss of any comfort they can renounce for his sake (Isaiah 57:18–19). For this and the like reasons we may conceive the Lord as Creator, recommended to the remembrance of men who have the strongest lusts unsubdued and apprehend the greatest difficulty in renouncing the pleasures of them: 'Remember now thy Creator in the days of thy youth.'

3. It is not possible to get the heart drawn from earthly delights, and so engaged to the fear and obedience of the Lord, unless it be stayed upon him and replenished with frequent thoughts of his properties, which will bring in so much holy awe of him and such apprehensions of sweetness to be had in him that sinful pleasures will appear to be but husks or swine's food in comparison to it. And the soul will not dare to feed upon these husks if it has clear and frequent thoughts of the sovereignty and power of God the Creator. For having dissuaded from carnal pleasures in the close of the former chapter, and being afterward in this [i.e. later in this chapter] to recommend to the study of living in the fear of obedience of the Lord as the only way to true happiness, he here presses this 'Remember thy Creator' as the best way to divert the heart from the one and engage it to the other.

4. The time of youth is the fittest time for the study of reconciliation with God and walking in his fear and obedience.

At that age the wit [mind] and memory are ripest and the affections most vigorous, and therefore should be spent in that study which only is worthy of them—especially considering that it is but just with God to reject men, though they should offer themselves to him, when they have given the flower of their time, wit, strength and affections to the service of Satan and their lusts, and that, if he should accept them, the remembrance of their misspent youth will be extremely heavy and will readily occasion in the best people fears of off-casting [being rejected] in old age (compare Psalm 25:7 with Psalm 71:18). 'Remember now thy Creator in the days of thy youth.'

5. As there is a natural propensity in all to forget God and to shift [avoid] serious thoughts of him, and therefore all men have need of a remembrancer to mind [remind] them often of this great duty pressed in the text, so, of all others, young men are the most apt to forget God and put off serious thoughts of him and their own souls, their lusts being strongest and their hearts most capable [receptive] of the sweetness of earthly delights. Hence the ministers of Christ, though they have often the least hope of success in dealing with wanton, proud, insolent and furious youth [impetuous young people], yet they must press this duty upon them and urge them in the name of the Lord to make use of the present opportunity for it. 'Remember now thy Creator in the days of thy youth.'

6. However days of affliction, old age and infirmity may be good days to those who have made their peace with God (Habakkuk 3:17; Romans 8:28), yet they are evil days in themselves, and will prove no better than a begun hell to

## Verse 1—Making preparation

them who still defer the study of making their peace with God. For so the Preacher describes the times of affliction which befall men, especially toward death, calling the same 'evil days': 'While the evil days come not.'

7. While men have health and strength and immunity from trouble, they should be forecasting [foreseeing] evil days and unpleasant years, that so in the summer and harvest of youth and strength they may be making provision for the stormy winter of affliction and old age (Proverbs 10:9) by ensuring the pardon of their sins through the blood of Christ, which else [otherwise] will readily compass them about as unpardoned in such times (Psalm 49:5). And so they should be making clear their interest in God, which is the only consolation in evil days (Habakkuk 3:17). For Solomon supposes here every young man to have evil days and years of trouble before him, which he should forecast, and thereby be moved to prepare timeously for them. 'Remember now thy Creator in the days of thy youth, while the evil days come not, nor the years draw nigh, when thou shalt say, I have no pleasure in them.'

8. The Lord will once [one day] make earthly delights tasteless and loathsome to men before they go out of this life. He does it to the godly (2 Samuel 19:34–35), that divine consolations may relish the better [may be more agreeable] with them and they may long for the pleasures that are at his right hand. And to the wicked also (Daniel 5:5–6), that they may see their folly in satisfying themselves with these things only, which cannot give them any comfort when they have most need of it. And so the Lord often gains a testimony from both good and bad that earthly delights are unworthy to be

delighted in, for Solomon supposes here that there is a time for every man, in which he shall say, 'I have no pleasure in them.'

9. Christ's ministers should be so well acquainted with the language of dying men, both by their daily observing of the case of such men and their study of the Scriptures, which will inform them of it (Proverbs 5:11; 1 Thessalonians 5:3), that they may be able to inform men who have least mind of [who least consider] death what sentence they will pass in their own conscience and what language they shall readily utter to others concerning their sinful pleasures when they shall be drawing near to the gates of death, that so they may the more effectually prevail with them to renounce in time these sinful pleasures. For Solomon here represents [displays] to the voluptuous [sensual] young man, who is cheering up his heart in his sins and banishing the thoughts of death, what he shall say of his youthly [youthful] pleasures when sickness comes and death draws near: 'Thou shall say, I have no pleasure in them.'

# 2

# Declining comforts

Verse 2

*While the sun, or the light, or the moon, or the stars, be not darkened, nor the clouds return after the rain.*

THE Preacher here further describes negatively the fittest opportunity for the study of reconciliation and peace with God, and withal [in addition] he more particularly describes the miseries incident to old age, as to the loss of outward comforts and frequent returns of diseases at that time. This being clear, and generally agreed upon by interpreters to be the scope of this place, we need not be very anxious concerning the particular application of the allegories here made use of to set forth this purpose.

1. First, by the darkening of the sun, the light, the moon and stars may be safely understood the eclipsing or withdrawing of all earthly comforts (seeing the Scripture sets out a comfortless state this way) and it may comprehend particularly:

1) The darkening of the dying man's bodily eyes.
2) And so secondly [the darkening of] all external lights to him as to any comfort he may reap from them.
3) As also thirdly the decaying of his reason and such faculties of his soul as are in a manner answerable to the celestial lights.
4) And likewise, fourthly, the failing of all outward comforts, both greater and lesser. It is clear the loss of all these accompanies dying men, and so they may be all comprehended here as parts and enlargements of one and the same sense of the words.

2. Next, by the returning of the clouds after rain seems clearly to be understood that continual succession and frequent returning of one shower of trouble after another which befall dying men. And the allegory or similitude seems to be borrowed from the tempestuous and stormy seasons of the year, when it is not as in summer, that after a shower clears up again and becomes fair and warm, which represents the time of youth, in which ordinarily, after some fit of sickness and distemper, ease and health come again. But as it is in winter, after one shower the clouds presently [soon] gather for another, so it will be in the time of old age. As for that particular which many condescend upon [specify] as intended here, to wit, the frequent falling down of rheums [watery discharge from the nose] or catarrhs [mucus] from the head, like so many showers upon the lungs, that seems to be but one instance of this general, to wit, the frequent recurring of one fit of distemper after another, incident to dying men.

## Verse 2—Declining comforts

Hence learn:

1. It is not enough for men to have general apprehensions of their mortality and the certainty of their death, but it is necessary that their thoughts be stayed upon [settled on] the distinct and particular apprehension of the case they shall be in at that time, while the several pins of their tabernacle shall be a-loosing [in the process of being loosed], that by a serious and considered view of their case then they may be stirred up to provide suitable spiritual consolations against the removal of every one of their outward comforts. Therefore it is that Solomon, after a general intimation in the former verse that death and trouble are before men, comes here more particularly to lead them to distinct thoughts of the case they shall be in then: 'While the sun, or the light, or the moon, or the stars, be not darkened.'

2. The benefit of our eyes and of the light of the sun, as also our reason and other faculties of the soul, together with the comforts we have by the use of all these, are excellent mercies of God, and while they are continued with us do put us in a good capacity to prepare for death. While we have the use of our bodily eyes and our reason, we may contemplate the glorious works of God and read his Word, by which we may attain to the knowledge of God in Christ and fellowship with him. For this end all these lights—whether of our eyes, our reason, the external lights of heaven, or whatever may be set forth by these names—are given to us. For this is a part of the description of that opportunity to be made use of for remembering our Creator: 'While the sun, or the light, or the moon, or the stars, be not darkened.'

3. We should use our mercies and privileges which are common to us with other men, to wit, our bodily sight, our reason, and all other comforts which may be signified by the lights here mentioned, so as we may be still mindful of the decay and failing of them at death, and often think with ourselves what a comfort it will be to see by faith him that is invisible, favourable to us; to behold Christ, the Son of righteousness, shining in mercy upon us, and to have the day star, his Spirit, arising in our hearts (2 Peter 1:19), never to set again, even when all other lights and outward comforts will be darkened—the ensuring of which to ourselves should (according to Solomon's scope here) be our great study: 'While the sun, or the light, or the moon, or the stars, be not darkened.'

4. Although no man can promise to himself fair weather in this world, but ought to resolve for one shower of affliction after another, yet the Lord is pleased to give unto men, now and then, breathing times from outward troubles—and some seasons in which there is a clear sunshine after rain and no present appearance of trouble, that they may, with the greater tranquillity of spirit, prepare for the same. For it is here supposed that they may have some times of fair summer weather while the clouds do not return after the rain.

5. Every man may expect that frequent troubles shall assault him when old age comes and death draws near, like one shower pouring down immediately after another is over, till he is carried into eternity as with a flood (Psalm 90:5). For it is imported that it will be thus with him when death draws near, while his case, in some health, is thus described: 'Nor the clouds return after the rain.'

## Verse 2—Declining comforts

6. Every intermission [cessation] of trouble should be improved for making preparation for the last storm, by storing the heart with such thoughts of God reconciled to us in Christ as may prove comfortable to us when death comes. For this is a part of the description of the opportunity to be made use of for that end: while the clouds return not after the rain.

# 3

# A besieged castle

### Verse 3

*In the day when the keepers of the house shall tremble, and the strong men shall bow themselves, and the grinders cease because they are few, and those that look out of the windows be darkened.*

THE Preacher comes now to positively describe the time of the dissolution of this tabernacle as not so convenient an opportunity as the time of youth and health for making peace with God. And for this end he illustrates the case of a man assaulted by death by the similitude of a besieged house or castle, whose guards and watches [watchmen] become feeble and desert their duty.

1. As for the keepers of the house and the strong men, however, many parts of a man may be understood by these, whether the outward senses or the inward faculties, because they all look to the safety of the whole body. Yet it seems

## Verse 3—A Besieged Castle

most proper to take the keepers for the arms and hands, because they are most active to keep the rest of the body from hazard, and it is known that palsies and shakings agree best to them—and by the strong men to understand the thighs and legs, because the Scripture attributes feebleness, or bowing to these (Isaiah 35:3).

2. By the grinders are meant the teeth, which prepare and make small the food for the stomach; these cease from this duty, being few and unfit for it in old age.

3. And by these that look out at the windows are to be understood the eyes which stand in their holes, as watches in their towers, to espy hazards and advantages which may befall the body. The darkening here spoken of makes it clear that he speaks of the eyes and not of the other senses, though by consequence the decay of these brings along with it a decay of sight also.

Hence learn:

1. Man's body is of a wonderful constitution, and very curiously framed, like some stately edifice or garrison, having the arms and hands as keepers, which can move towards all the airths [points of the compass] for defending of it; the legs as strong men to carry it out of one country to another to escape hazard, which no castle has; the teeth for grinders, to prepare the food for it, and the eyes as watches to espy hazards, that they may be prevented. This house should be kept out [retained] for Christ's use, the temple of whose Spirit it is, and not rendered up to be a habitation for Satan and these armies of unclean lusts which are soldiers under him. All the

members [parts of the body] should be made use of as weapons of righteousness to keep it out against temptations as well as against outward hazards. For so does the wise man here set out this human body under the similitude of a stately house or fortified castle, while he says, 'The keepers of the house shall tremble, and the strong men shall bow themselves, and the grinders cease because they are few, and those that look out of the windows be darkened.'

2. Death, the king of terrors, will give such a sore assault to this house of the body that, let men defend and supply it as they will, it must be at last surrendered to worms and corruption to dwell in. They are happy who timeously make sure [secure] a house not made with hands for their better part, for they shall get this house again in a more glorious and durable condition. For it is here clearly held forth that, when death approaches, all the officers and servants of this great house shall be put from their employments. 'In the day when the keepers of the house shall tremble, and the strong men shall bow themselves.'

3. Men that are now acting [performing] wickedness with both their hands greedily, making them weapons of unrighteousness—whether to serve their own lusts in gluttony, drunkenness and other carnal ways, or to wrong others by oppression, shedding of innocent blood, and the like, in which the hands are mainly instrumental—ought to be put in mind of this, that there is a day certainly abiding [awaiting] them and swiftly coming upon them, in which these hands shall not be able to act after that manner, nay, not so much as to hold a drink to their own head for trembling. By these and the like considerations they may be moved to

## Verse 3—A Besieged Castle

make better use of them, to stretch them often out in works of charity, to lift them often up in prayer and praise and employ them in such other lawful exercises as may be comfortable [comforting] to them in death. For every branch of this description of the decay of men's bodies ought to be improved for pressing the main use of preparation for death, and has its own peculiar influence for that end, so men might have peace and comfort 'in the day when the keepers of the house shall tremble'.

4. While men are able to stand or walk, it concerns them to look how they use their legs, that they might not be proud of their strength while they have it, that they do not employ it in walking after their lusts but in running the way of God's commands. And that they often bow their 'strong men' to God in prayer for strength to other duties; so they may make sure to themselves that they shall have below them the everlasting arms of him whose legs are as pillars of marble and his rod and staff to support them in the day that the 'strong men' bow themselves. For, this part of the description—to wit, the decay of the strength of the legs—requires some suitable preparation for it.

5. As the wisdom and goodness of God should be much acknowledged in giving men such durable and fit instruments as their teeth for grinding and preparing their food—and these same should not be used in making provision for the flesh, to fulfil the lusts thereof, but in eating for strength to serve the Giver of them—so, while men have the use of these, they should look upon them as fading, and consider that as they did not bring them with them into the world, so it is likely they should carry few of them hence, if so be they

live to old age. And while these grinders are able to exerce their office [perform their function], men should be careful to feed upon Jesus Christ the Bread of Life, which their ordinary food should represent and mind [remind] them of. For this will be the true preparation for this day when 'the grinders cease because they are few'.

6. As men's bodily eyes are to be highly prized and holily used [used in a holy way] in reading the Word and beholding the works of God, for bringing into their souls matter of his praise, and not to be made emissaries for bringing in temptations and fuel to men's lusts (1 Peter 2:14), so while we enjoy them we should often remember the time when we shall be deprived of them, and by the thoughts of them be moved to use them well, considering that the abuse of them will make the want [lack] of them very grievous. For the Preacher here minds men of the darkening of them as a motive to prepare for death by the right use of them, and to study to get the second sight which is faith, beholding him that is invisible reconciled through Christ: so there shall be true comfort in the day when those that look out at the windows shall be darkened.

# 4

# Declining strength

Verse 4

*And the doors shall be shut in the streets, when the sound of the grinding is low, and he shall rise up at the voice of the bird, and all the daughters of music shall be brought low.*

HE goes on to describe further the dissolution of the earthly house of our tabernacle in several particulars, of which four are in this verse.

1. The first is the shutting of the doors in the streets, in which words there seems to be a metaphor taken from the custom of these houses where sick persons are: they keep closed the doors which open toward the streets, that the sick may not be disturbed by any going out or coming in. And it may signify this much in general that, while death is drawing near, correspondence [interaction] between the dying man and the world is now given up, as men shut their doors at night when they are making toward their rest. And so the

words have a truth literally in regard that visits become ordinarily a burden to dying men. The doors also may be taken metaphorically for these organs or instruments of the body—such as the mouth, lips, throat and the like—whereby speech is conveyed to others and meat passes down to the stomach. These doors are shut when the dying man becomes unable to put forth speech or to make use of meat and drink.

2. As for the next expression, 'when the sound of the grinding is low', there is in it also a metaphor taken from the decay of the sound of mills, when the water fails. And it is most clear to understand this as holding forth the consequent [consequence] of the ceasing of the grinders spoken of in the former verse: because the teeth are few, they make no such sound in breaking the food as they were wont to do when the man had health and strength. And this, according to the construction of the words in our translation, has connection with the former as the cause of it: the doors formerly explained are shut where there is no power in the teeth to prepare food for the stomach.

3. By the third expression, 'he shall rise up at the voice of the bird', is not meant that the dying man shall be able at all to rise, but that his weakness is such through the coldness and emptiness of his stomach and the dryness of his brain, that he shall get no sound sleep at all, but the least noise—suppose it were of some little bird—shall put him off his rest.

4. And by the fourth expression, 'the daughters of music shall be brought low', is meant that all the organs or instruments of the voice and hearing—by which men did either make melody or pleasant speech to others, or did delight in

## VERSE 4—DECLINING STRENGTH

such made by others—shall be then so weakened, that they shall neither hear others nor be heard by them.

Hence learn:

1. While men are able to keep up society [keep company] with others, to go out of doors to them or admit them into their houses, and to speak to and hear one another, they should labour to improve that correspondence for the advantage of their own and others' souls, to edify and be edified by one another, remembering that the day is coming when they will love to have the doors of their house that look to the streets shut, lest their sinful companions may come in to vex them. And though they were with them, they will not be able to open the doors of their lips to correspond any more with them. How comfortable will it then be to have Christ dwelling in the heart by faith, and to be keeping up correspondence with him by prayer and praise, which is the true preparation for this case, when 'the doors shall be shut in the streets'.

2. It will be a great affliction to men when they shall find themselves to stand in need of creature comforts and have these beside them, and yet have no power to use them. And therefore, while they have as much strength as to break their own bread, they should eat in sobriety, and with thankfulness employ the strength they receive by their food in God's service. So they shall prepare for and have comfort in this time, when the sound of the grinding shall be low.

3. Sound sleep, without such distemper of body or horror of conscience as mars the same [disturbs sleep], is a great mercy,

which the Lord bestows upon his own whenever he sees it good for them (Psalm 117:2 and 84:11). So, while men enjoy it, they should use it soberly and employ all the refreshment they get by it in the service of the Giver: labouring so to walk in the daytime that their sleep may be sanctified, their reins[13] may teach them in the night season (Psalm 16:7), and they may rise early for holy exercises (Psalm 5:3), that whenever they awake they may be still with God (Psalm 139:18). And if at any time sleep departs from them, they may then think upon and prepare for the case they shall be in when death draws near. For he speaks of this as a part of the affliction of dying men, and minds men in health of it, that they may thus prepare for it, when they 'shall rise up at the voice of the bird'.

4. As man's tongue is given him for glorifying his Maker, his voice and all the organs of it for cheering his own and others' hearts in his praises, his ears to take in the joyful sound of the gospel for refreshing of his heart, so while he has the use of these instruments, his tongue and ears, he should be careful so to employ them. He should often let the Lord hear his voice in prayer and praise, seeing the same is pleasant to him (Song of Solomon 2:14). He should be much in edifying discourses with others, which are also sweet to the Lord (Malachi 3:16), and nothing taken up [in no way taken up] with carnal mirth or music, that so, when he shall not be able to speak to or hear others, he may be making melody to the Lord in his heart and may hear his Spirit speaking peace there. For this is the true preparation (comprehended under

---

[13] Literally, kidneys. The term is used metaphorically to express the seat of the emotions.

## Verse 4—Declining strength

that direction—verse 1) for such a case as this, when 'all the daughters of music shall be brought low'.

# 5

# Increasing fears

Verse 5

*Also when they shall be afraid of that which is high, and fears shall be in the way, and the almond tree shall flourish, and the grasshopper shall be a burden, and desire shall fail: because man goeth to his long home, and the mourners go about the streets.*

HERE is a further description of the case that men shall be in when death is drawing near to them, held forth in several expressions.

1. The first two—they 'shall be afraid of that which is high' and 'fears shall be in the way'—are to the same purpose. Both signify the want of strength and courage and the fearful apprehensions incident to dying men. Particularly by 'that which is high' may be meant any step of their way which is higher than another, and the least stumbling block in their way, which to a crazy decayed man (such as Solomon here

## VERSE 5—INCREASING FEARS

describes) is matter of fear lest it make him fall, considering how hurtful a fall may prove to him and how hardly [with difficulty] he would be set to his feet again. And so the words suppose the dying man yet able to step up and down, as some will be till very near the time of their removal. Or by 'that which is high' and the 'fears in the way' may be meant the least trouble, were it but the weight of a hand above the dying person, or any action about them which is to them terrible, and makes them fear lest it increase their pain.

2. Next, by the 'flourishing of the almond tree' may be meant the hastening of the person's death—so the allegory or similitude is used (Jeremiah 1:11)—because that tree flourishes near the end of winter, and consequently it may signify also the decay of their strength, whereof grey hairs, which resemble in colour the flourishes of the almond tree, are a sign. As on the contrary this same heavenly writer sets forth the vigour and strength of youth, in a spiritual sense, by the temples (where grey hairs first appear) compared to a piece of pomegranate which is ruddy and white (Song of Solomon 6:7). Or the similitude may have this sense (which is to the same purpose), that the blood being now retired [drawn back] toward the heart of the dying man, the pale white clay [the pallor of the body] appears like the flourishes of the almond tree.

3. The fourth expression, 'the grasshopper shall be a burden', also signifies the great decay of strength, in so much that the lightest thing (were it but a gnat or grasshopper lighting upon the face of the dying man) shall be a burden to him, and yet he shall not be able to put it away.

4. The fifth is (in more plain and proper terms) that desire—to wit, after all earthly objects, whether lawful, such as meat, drink, marriage, delight, and the like, or unlawful, such as revengeful, ambitious, lustful desires reckoned out (1 John 2:16)—shall now cool and be quite extinguished.

To all which he subjoins [adds] a reason, 'because man goeth to his long home', or as the original is, to the house of eternity or ages, whereby is meant that estate, in which the soul must be eternally, without any further change.

5. And for the last expression, 'the mourners going about the streets', the meaning of it is that the man, being now given over as dead, the persons made use of in these times to solemnize the funerals were already convening and waiting on [waiting for the funerals to begin]. Or alternatively, the dying man's friends are now going out from him and already beginning their mourning for his death. Before this time comes, it is wisdom to make sure work of reconciliation with God in Christ, and to provide some suitable consolation for the spirit while the body shall be in this condition.

Hence learn:

1. As long as men have that much natural strength and courage to walk up and down without fear of the ordinary impediments and stumbling blocks that lie in their way, it concerns them to employ their strength well to walk in fear of offending the Lord all the day long (Proverbs 23:17), to make sure their peace with him, who is most high, that he may not be a terror to them in the day of evil (Jeremiah 17:17), to have their faith of an interest in God so well fixed

## VERSE 5—INCREASING FEARS

that they may not fear to walk through the valley of the shadow of death (Psalm 23:4), to lay up in time some suitable consolation against the continuance and extremity of temporal trouble, the terror and pain of death, and every other thing that may be fearful to them in their way to eternity. And to have so much use of sanctified reason and faith as may discover [reveal] everything that may present itself as terrible to the natural man to be no cause of fear banishing faith.[14] For this is true preparation for the case here described, when man 'shall be afraid of that which is high, and fears shall be in the way'.

2. As men should always look upon death as hasting toward them, and so learn to die daily (1 Corinthians 15:31), so especially when signs of the decay of their natural strength appear upon them they should then esteem themselves near the end of the winter of this life, and labour to have grace so lively that (in regard of the exercise of it) they may flourish even in old age (Psalm 92:12). And study to have their hoary head found as a crown of glory to them in the way of righteousness (Proverbs 16:31). And while they are young and strong, not to glory in such excrementitious [worthless] things as their hair, which will shortly be like the almond tree. So they shall prepare for this state set forth under this similitude: 'and the almond tree shall flourish'.

3. Men that have most strength of body should look upon that as a very fading thing, and so not to be trusted in or employed in serving their lusts (Isaiah 5:22) but in bearing

---

[14] Nisbet speaks of faith overcoming natural fears relating to death, which could easily give opportunity for unbelief.

Christ's yoke, whether of duties (Matthew 11:29) or crosses (Lamentations 3:27), and so they may have true comfort. And so they may cast their burden upon the Lord with confidence that he shall sustain them, when this shall be their case which this allegorical expression holds out: 'and the grasshopper shall be a burden'.

4. God will once [one day] before men go off this world cut off all their desires from earthly objects, so that wicked men, finding themselves to abhor these sinful delights which once they did so ardently desire, may be the more convinced of their folly and madness, and that the godly, finding their lawful earthly delights loathsome to them, may rejoice that delights of a better nature are abiding them. The consideration of this should move all to mortify their sinful desires and moderate their lawful desires after earthly things, and to have their hearts filled with heavenly desires, which shall be satisfied and yet shall never fail (Philippians 1:23). For this is the best preparation for this condition: 'desires shall fail'.

5. When ministers make use of allegories to illustrate the Truth, they ought to join with them such plain expressions of the meaning of them as may clear the scope they aim at, lest continued allegories breed vanity and wantonness of the wit, divert the mind from delighting in the simplicity of the Truth, and form in the heart misapprehensions of the Truth. Therefore Solomon in the midst of these allegories inserts some plain and proper expressions, such as this is: 'desire shall fail'.

6. Though the men of this world (whose best portion is in this present life) promise to themselves a perpetuity of

enjoying earthly things (Psalm 49:12; 2 Peter 3:4), yet they shall find themselves within a little [short time] miserably disappointed: they shall find that this is not their home. It would be wisdom to look upon their mansions here as short [temporary] homes to them, and upon themselves as strangers and pilgrims, that so they might give all diligence to ensure to themselves everlasting habitations. For, when death comes, 'man goeth to his long [permanent] home'.

7. After death there is no change of the state of souls as to their misery or felicity: they must for ever remain either with Satan in his prison, or with Christ in his Father's house where there are many mansions. And consequently there can be no such place as the purgatory which the Romanists dream of. For thus Solomon describes the state of man after death: he 'goeth to his long home', or to his house of eternity or ages.

8. While men have comfortable society with their friends, God would have them thinking upon the day when they must leave them mourning behind them, that by the consideration of this they may be stirred up to make conscience of duty to them, that so they may not part with them with a conscience accusing them for neglect of this, and that their friends' loss by their removal may be compensed [recompensed] by the biding [abiding] fruit of their pains [diligent labours] toward them, and they may have no ground to mourn for them, as those that have no hope. So shall the dying man have comfort within, 'when the mourners go about the streets'.

# 6

# Physical weakening

Verse 6

*Or ever the silver cord be loosed, or the golden bowl be broken, or the pitcher be broken at the fountain, or the wheel broken at the cistern.*

ALTHOUGH this verse may be understood literally—and in that sense may be usefully applied to the scope that men should remember their Creator, which is to make sure work of their peace with him before they be deprived of all their outward ornaments and necessary commodities of this life, or the instruments of their employment, whatever it may be—yet it seems most suitable to the strain of the Preacher in the former purpose to look upon the words as containing so many sweet allegories or similitudes to set forth the decay or dissolution of the most noble parts of this earthly tabernacle.

VERSE 6—PHYSICAL WEAKENING

The similitudes are borrowed from a fountain or well, about which is built some curious engine [mechanism] for drawing up the water, with a silver cord or chain to let down a golden bowl or pitcher, or some such vessel, to lift up the water. This similitude fitly points out the human body, which has a fountain of natural life and spirits within it, and so many excellent instruments to convoy and impart these to the several parts of the body, all of which at death will be loosed and broken to pieces.

This general sense might be satisfactory and useful as to the scope, which is to stir up men to remember their Creator before these noble parts are decayed. And it may be thought safe to enquire no further anent [concerning] the particulars intended by every part of the similitude, considering that it seems now to be very uncertain by what names these noble parts of the body (the heart, brain, liver, and the like) were called and distinguished one from another among the Hebrews in Solomon's time, and by what similitudes they were set out, which make great diversity among interpreters in expounding and applying of them.

And considering also that there are several of these parts, which may be represented by diverse parts of this similitude, yet we shall mention what is most universally agreed upon, to be pointed at by the particulars of the allegory here made use of.

1. And first, by the silver cord is meant the marrow of the backbone, compared to a silver cord, because much of the strength of the body lies in it, in so much as without it men would creep upon the earth as worms do, and because in

colour it resembles a silver cord. The loosing of it is the weakening of it. When the spirits withdraw from it, it becomes cold and loses its force [strength]. The similitude may also signify some of the prime arteries or strings of the heart [blood vessels], which convey the vital spirits from there to the liver and other parts of the body.[15]

2. Secondly, the 'golden bowl' is taken from that yellow thin skin containing the brain within the skull, which is broken when the pores of it are much opened to let in the air, as falls out [happens] near the time of death.

3. Thirdly, the pitcher at the fountain is thought to point out a great hollow vein, somewhat in form or figure like a pitcher, which receives nutriment from the liver (here called the cistern), now turned by the liver into blood, to be conveyed to the rest of the members, and this is broken when it is obstructed, or the operation and office [function] of it is impeded near the time of death.

4. Fourthly, by the wheel at the cistern are meant the lungs, the prime instruments of the breath and voice, which are set out by this similitude because, like the wheel of a fountain, they are still [continuously] in motion, drawing down and

---

[15] It will be appreciated that medical knowledge in Nisbet's day made mistaken assumptions about the structure and function of organs. It was believed that air mixed with blood in the heart and created a vital essence which was conveyed to various organs. When it was reached the brain it was converted into 'animal spirits'—the word 'animal' meaning 'having breath'—which were transmitted by nerves to all parts of the body. Nisbet's interpretation of this part of the chapter is affected by these prevailing views of anatomy and physiology.

## Verse 6—Physical Weakening

sending up the breath again, as the wheel is still sending down, or drawing up the bucket. This wheel is broken at the cistern when, through the abundance of watery humours or phlegm filling the stomach, they cease from their motion and operation, and so bring death.

Now the first words of the chapter are to be knit with this, as with all the former to this purpose: remember thy Creator before this case come, and timeously make peace with him, that you may have peace in this day.

Hence learn:

1. Men should not despise human learning and the knowledge or science of natural things, if it were for no more but to help them to understand the fabric of their own bodies. And although every man's gift is not to be laid aside as to the public employing [use] of it, because he wants [lacks] such-and-such a measure of human learning, seeing the Lord has made eminent use of some who wanted it (Acts 4:13), as he has done also of others who have been eminently endued with it (Acts 7:22 and 22:3), yet every man's short-sightedness in it should humble him and move him to bestow some of his time for attaining to it, especially considering that man's body is so wonderful a piece of artifice [workmanship] that, without the help of these sciences which describe them, such Scriptures as this can hardly be made clear. 'Ere the silver cord be loosed, or the golden bowl be broken, or the pitcher be broken at the fountain, or the wheel broken at the cistern.'

2. The Lord has wisely ordered that death should assault and take down this tabernacle of our body by degrees, and loose at leisure the several pins of it, first weakening the outworks [outer defensive walls] and then setting upon the inward, that every stroke and assault may be a warning for a further one, and that when men find their hands trembling or their legs enfeebled, their eyes dim or their ears dull of hearing, they may prepare for an assault upon the heart and other noble parts. For after Solomon has described the dissolution of several other parts of the body, he comes here to the inmost and most noble parts of it, that men may be stirred up to remember their Creator at last, ere 'the silver cord be loosed, or the golden bowl be broken'.

3. All the organs of the body, especially the more noble parts of it, are very excellent pieces of work, and to be so esteemed of, not so much for the substance of them as for the divine art which is manifested in the framing of them and the excellent uses they serve for. And therefore both these and the powers and faculties of the soul (which reside in and act by these) are to be used holily. Man's strength—here mainly held out by the silver cord—should be esteemed more precious than to be spent upon his lusts. He should beware of filling this golden bowl—his brain, in which these excellent faculties (his imagination and memory) have their prime residence—with unclean, ambitious, revengeful speculations and such like immoralities, and by intemperance and excess to spoil this pitcher, corrupt this cistern, and break this wheel (his liver, lungs and other parts, which may be signified by these similitudes) and so do what he can to be his own destroyer. Therefore these parts of the body are set out here by such elegant metaphors or similitudes bor-

## Verse 6—Physical Weakening

rowed from very precious things: the silver cord, the golden bowl, the pitcher and the wheel.

4. These parts of the body which are most excellent and durable are to be looked upon as very brittle and fading, and therefore a house not made with hands is to be ensured [we are to make sure of a house not made with hands]. This frail body is to be respected and cared for only so far as it may be the more instrumental in doing the Lord service while we have it. Therefore the most noble parts of the body are here represented by a golden bowl, a pitcher and a wheel.

5. While men have some measure of health and strength, they should consider that it will be no fit time for making their peace and acquaintance with God in Christ when death shall be loosing the last pins of their tabernacle—these powers and faculties of the soul, which are mainly active in knowing, believing, loving, and praising the Lord, being then in the process of decaying. And therefore they should think it their true wisdom timeously to remember their Creator in the days of their youth and strength, ere 'the silver cord be loosed, or the golden bowl be broken, or the pitcher be broken at the fountain, or the wheel broken at the cistern'.

# 7

# Beyond death

Verse 7

*Then shall the dust return to the earth, as it was: and the spirit shall return unto God who gave it.*

SOLOMON having at length described the dissolution of the earthly house of our tabernacle after death, he gives here a sum of man's future state after death, in reference to the two principal parts of which he is made up.

1. And first, for his body, which he calls dust, because it was formed out of the dust (Genesis 2:7) and, being separate from the soul, is the most vile and loathsome piece of dust of any other. He says it returns to the dust, because it is ordinarily laid there, to remain till the resurrection, and because it is in effect the same substance with it.

2. And next, for his more noble part, his soul (called here the spirit, because of its immaterial substance and its resemblance to God, the Father of spirits) returns to him who gave

## Verse 7—Beyond Death

it. There is no ground to think he speaks only of the souls of the godly, but rather of the common state of the spirits of all men after death. And neither is there any necessity to think that therefore every soul must go to heaven, seeing the Scripture is so clear to the contrary. But every soul is said to return to God, because in the very moment of its separation from the body, it must sist [present][16] itself before him, the Supreme Judge, to be eternally disposed of according to his pleasure, who will sentence it according to the state it shall be found in at death. And these considerations also have great influence in exciting [inciting] men timeously to make their peace with God, that he may favourably entertain their spirits at death and they may lay down their bodies in the dust in hope of a glorious resurrection. And this is the reference which this verse has to the scope expressed in the first words of the chapter.

Hence learn:

1. Although our bodies have some beauty and majesty imprinted on them while the soul resides in them and they are acted [actuated] by it (for which cause they were set out by these excellent similitudes formerly mentioned), yet of themselves they are but dust, and when the soul is separate from them will appear to be very loathsome clay. The thought of this should keep men from being proud of their bodily strength or beauty (Jeremiah 9:23). It should make them admire the Lord's condescending to have correspondence with such dust (Genesis 28:27), his marvellous art and

---

[16] Sist has the specific connotation of presenting oneself for trial at a court.

power in framing so beautiful a piece of work as our bodies of [from] the dust (Psalm 139:24), especially his assuming so frail a being as a human body in a personal union with the Deity (Psalm 8:4), etc. It should be made use of as a ground of confidence to obtain pity and help from him to frail dust (Psalm 103:14) and of submission to the hardest dispensations (Isaiah 45:9). It should make us careful to get the ornament of his grace, which makes base dust truly beautiful (1 Peter 3:4). It should banish the fear of all flesh which is but dust like ourselves (Isaiah 51:7:8) and should make us long for the time when Christ shall change our vile bodies and make them like his glorious body (Philippians 3:21)—all of which are the uses the Scripture makes of this consideration, that we are dust.

2. The bodies of men at death do not go (as their spirits go) to that state in which they must be eternally, but the Lord has so ordered as they were at first taken out of the earth, so they must go there for a time, that in that way he may prove and exercise his people's faith concerning the resurrection. For, he says, 'The dust shall return to the earth as it was.'

3. The souls of men do not die or go to corruption as their bodies do, but subsist [continue to exist] after their separation from the body, which should make men careful to see to their eternal well-being, for Solomon here, supposing the body, or dust, to be gone to the earth, he speaks of the soul or spirit as now subsisting. By this it appears that the immortality of the soul has been preached to the ancient Churches: 'The spirit returns to God who gave it.'

4. Men do not receive their souls from their parents as they do their bodies, and they are not formed of any pre-existent matter, as the spirits are which beasts have (Genesis 1:20), but are created of nothing, and immediately [directly] infused into the body by the Lord, for, saith the Preacher, 'The spirit shall return to God who gave it.'

5. Our spirits are God's free gift, and therefore all their powers and faculties ought to be employed to the honour of the giver (Romans 11:26). He is to be depended on and acknowledged for the preservation of them (Job 10:12). And all crosses [tribulations] upon body or spirit are to be submitted to (Hebrews 12:9). For he says, 'The spirit returns to God who gave it.'

6. As the spirits of men, even the greatest on earth, are in God's hand to be moved by him while they are in the body as he pleases (Proverbs 21:1), so when they go out of the body they must sist themselves before him to be disposed of at his pleasure. He will throw the spirits of the wicked into the lake that flames with fire and brimstone, and will bind up the spirits of the godly as his jewels in the bundle of life, for in reference to both, this is verified: 'The spirit shall return to God who gave it.'

# 8

# A considered verdict

Verse 8

*Vanity of vanities, saith the Preacher; all is vanity.*

IN this and the following verses is contained the last part of the chapter and the close of the whole book, in which the Preacher briefly sums up and, by several arguments, commends the purpose contained in it, which for method's cause [sake] we may take up in four articles or heads of doctrine.

The first, which is in this verse, contains the sum of the first principal part of the book, namely, that all created things, and human endeavours about them, are vain or insufficient for leading a man to his true happiness. And this having been frequently held out before is here necessarily repeated, that all may assent unto it as a truth now abundantly proved, and which the Preacher himself loved to meditate upon and write again and again. And with this repeating of it, he mentions his calling to be a preacher as that which should gain

## Verse 8—A Considered Verdict

weight to every truth delivered by him, and to this in particular.

Beside what has been observed from this purpose before, we may learn:

1. Necessary truths must not be cast by [thrown aside] after they are clear to us and sufficiently proved to be truths by many arguments. And they will not become loathsome to a holy mind, but ought to be entertained and meditated upon till we find motions [inclinations] suitable to them wakened in our hearts and some fruits in our practice answerable to them, which may evidence [show] we do truly know and believe them. And the more clear such truths are to a gracious soul, the sweeter they will grow, and the more delight the soul will have to dwell upon them. Therefore Solomon, after he has fully proved and cleared this truth and frequently asserted it, he here again represents the same to his own heart and others: 'Vanity of vanities, saith the Preacher; all is vanity.'

2. So prone are our hearts to wander after earthly delights as our only happiness that, even after they have been in some measure divorced from these, there is great need often to view the vanity of these things, as we desire to keep our hearts alienated from them and in love with that true sweetness which is to be had in communion with God. While we are in this life we are like children newly weaned, very ready to renew old acquaintance with the breasts. Therefore after frequently repeating this truth along [throughout] this treatise of [about] mortification, Solomon repeats it here again in the close of it, so that he may keep his heart alienated

from idols: 'Vanity of vanities, saith the Preacher; all is vanity.'

3. When ministers have sufficiently proved, illustrated and made use of the truth proposed by them to be handled, it is no vain repetition for them to represent the same truth in the very terms in which they did propose it at first, that by the blessing of God upon their proofs, illustrations and uses of it, it may now at last have more hearty acceptance and take deeper impression than could be expected at first. For so Solomon here repeats the truth he proposed in the entry [beginning] of this book, after he has cleared, proved and made use of the same: 'Vanity of vanities.'

4. When men see holiness in the beauty of it, sin in the hazard of it, and death in the certainty and terror of it, they cannot but see the vanity of earthly delights considered as the object of man's happiness; they cannot but see the emptiness and insufficiency of them in order to that end, seeing they distract the heart from the study of holiness and mar preparation for death. And consequently, men that banish thoughts of death and neglect the study of holiness cannot but be ravished with earthly delights as the only substantial things worthy of their heart and to be sought as their chief good. For we may safely conceive Solomon here (after many sweet precepts concerning the study of holiness, and lively representations of death to his own heart and others) to have got a new sight of the vanity of earthly things, and to invite others to pass sentence on them with him: 'Vanity of vanities, saith the Preacher; all is vanity.'

5. A man that has a call to preach the Truth of God should esteem more of it than of the most honourable outward relation or title he can have beside. He should carry the thoughts of God's calling and entrusting of him along in his heart, to make him confident of furniture [being supplied] even to the end of his employment. And people also should frequently remember the calling of sent ministers, that the truths delivered may have the greater weight as coming to them from God's commissioned officers. For, as Solomon took this for his first stile [title] in the beginning of his book, even while he was reckoning out some others, so he mentions it alone in the close as his main encouragement, and that which should mainly gain respect to his message: 'Vanity of vanities, saith the Preacher.'

6. When we have gone through many particular instances of these earthly delights in which men place their happiness, and have attained to convincing proofs of the vanity and insufficiency of them for that end, we ought then to raise our hearts to an assent to the truth of the general [general statement] that all of that sort are vanity, and not leave room still to Satan to keep our perverse hearts in suspense and expectation that there may be some earthly delight which we have not yet seen, more worthy than the rest, and so keep us off all our time from seeking happiness in that in which it can only be found. For after Solomon has confuted [proved to be false] many particular instances of these things in which men ordinarily seek their happiness, he now asserts the general, and holds out to all for their assent unto it: 'All is vanity.'

# 9

# The diligent preacher

### Verse 9

*And moreover, because the preacher was wise, he still taught the people knowledge; yea, he gave good heed, and sought out, and set in order many proverbs.*

THE second article or conclusion of this book contains a commendation of the purpose contained in it, and this has three branches. The first is from the Preacher himself, whose qualifications and pains are set forth in several particulars in this verse.

1. He had a good stock of wisdom, both immediately infused (1 Kings 4:29) and acquired by his extraordinary pains (Ecclesiastes 1:13).

2. He improved the same [the stock of wisdom] well for the instruction of the Church in all ages, especially these under his charge, here called 'the people'.

## Verse 9—The Diligent Preacher

3. He was very assiduous and constant in this work. He still taught, either by frequent preaching and exhortation, as a public officer of the Church (such as he was) should do (2 Timothy 4:2), or by putting other ministers to their duty and encouraging them in it, as a religious king like him should do (2 Chronicles 7:8–9), or by writing Scripture as an extraordinary prophet,[17] in which respect he, being dead, yet speaks and still teaches the people knowledge.

4. He did not rest upon any measure he had received, but gave good heed—or as the word in the original is, 'he weighed everything in the balance'—and sought out carefully more and more of the knowledge of God and of man's duty, that he might edify the Church.

5. He wisely ordered [placed in order] and digested the purpose he delivered.

6. He condescended upon a variety of matter suitable to many cases of the people.

7. He contrived [skilfully devised] this in such short and grave sentences, here called proverbs, as are apt to gain esteem and have prevalence [mastery] in the minds of men, as the word rendered 'proverbs' signifies: 'He set in order many proverbs.'

Hence learn:

1. Though the worth or qualifications of instruments can

---

[17] 'Extraordinary' is here used in the sense of 'specially appointed' or 'not according to the usual order'.

add nothing to the authority of the Truth of God, which is of itself worthy of all acceptation, whoever may carry it, yet so ready are people to lay hold upon everything that may but seem to be a ground of casting at [spurning] Truth that the vessels that carry it need not only to be without spot and blemish, but also adorned with such accomplishments as may make them lovely to people, that so there may be no ground from them to cast at [spurn] their message. For here the Spirit of God finds it necessary to commend the vessel that carried the treasure in this book to the Church, thereby to gain the more acceptance to it: 'And moreover, because the preacher was wise, he still taught the people knowledge; yea, he gave good heed, and sought out, and set in order many proverbs.'

2. As every Christian is bound humbly to avow the graces and gifts of God bestowed upon him, when the glory of God and the encouragement and edification of others require it, so it is especially suitable for ministers, when their intention is honest and sincere, namely to make Truth, not themselves only, in esteem. As they should be ready to declare themselves sensible [aware] of and humble for their failings, when it may glorify God or edify others, so they should also be to [have to] avow what graces God has given them, especially their qualifications for their calling, when the Lord has borne testimony to that by his blessing upon their labours. They must not so fear the suspicion of self-seeking as always to conceal the Lord's liberality toward them, but whenever it may serve to make way for his Truth, they ought humbly to declare it, as here this exemplary preacher does. 'And moreover, because the preacher was

## VERSE 9—THE DILIGENT PREACHER

wise, he still taught the people knowledge; yea, he gave good heed, and sought out, and set in order many proverbs.'

3. The greater measure of gifts (especially of knowledge and understanding of the matters of God) any man has attained to, the more careful he should be to communicate it for the good of others in his place and station, this being the end for which they are given (1 Corinthians 12:7). And the same is rewarded as if it were gain and advantage to God (Matthew 25:21), as likewise the communication of our gifts is the way to make them grow (Proverbs 11:25). For Solomon did therefore teach the people knowledge because he was wise, and the words may be rendered 'The greater abundance of wisdom he had, the more he taught the people knowledge.'

4. Albeit Christ's ministers cannot be always about the actual discharge of the duties of their calling, yet they ought to be very assiduous and frequent in them, and in some sense still about their work, gathering variety of matter fit to be communicated to the people (Matthew 13:52), keeping their hearts always in a right frame for the delivery of it (Proverbs 16:23) and watching all opportunities for communicating it (2 Timothy 4:2). And when they do not have the ability or opportunity to teach, their practice and carriage [habitual behaviour] must still teach the people knowledge (1 Timothy 4:12). For so Solomon here sets forth himself at the direction of the Spirit of God, as an example to all preachers: 'Because the preacher was wise, he still taught the people knowledge.'

5. They that are most able to teach others should still be scholars themselves, not only diligent hearers of other

preachers, that they may learn more, but accurate searchers for all means and opportunities of profiting in knowledge, there being still more knowledge to be had (Philippians 3:13) and success promised to the sincere seeker (Hosea 6:3). For though Solomon was wise and able to teach the people knowledge, yet he was not so satisfied with his measure as to become lazy or give over further pains for more: 'Yea, he gave good heed, and sought out, and set in order many proverbs.'

6. We should neither rashly receive nor vent anything for Truth till first we have weighed and pondered the same in the balance of the sanctuary by the exercise of sanctified reason, comparing it with the Scripture, considering what particular truths are most fitting for the people we have to do with and what are the fittest opportunities of delivering them. For so did Solomon: 'he gave good heed'—the word signifies to weigh in a balance—and he 'sought out', which signifies to search very accurately and carefully. And both may be referred either to what he himself received from others, or to what he gave out to others.

7. Even these of the Lord's servants who were immediately furnished with gifts for their employment, and infallibly assisted in the exercise of them were not exeemed [exempted] from ordinary pains and diligence to clear themselves more and more concerning the truths revealed to them, and to find out the fittest way and season of delivering these truths to the people (see 1 Peter 1:10). How then should ordinary ministers of meaner parts [talents] and gifts stretch their abilities to the utmost, and improve much of their time in prayer and reading, for increase of their gifts and fitness

## Verse 9—The Diligent Preacher

for the exercise of them, seeing such a man as Solomon was thus exercised? 'He gave good heed, and sought out, and set in order many proverbs.'

8. There is no form of speech that can be imagined prevalent [to prevail] with reasonable creatures but the Lord has condescended upon [consented to] it in his Word, where we find songs and lamentations, plain language and parables, large insisting [ample insistence] upon one purpose, and proverbs, which are short sentences cleared by similitudes, and so apt to prevail and have dominion (as the word 'proverb' signifies) in the minds of men. 'He set in order many proverbs.'

9. As the cases of the Lord's people are various, and difficulties, duties, temptations and consolations are many, so the Lord's Word is fitted for them all. It is divided into many parcels, and every one that handles it should labour to enrich himself with much of it, that he may bring forth variety of it to people according to their need. For, so did Solomon: 'He gave good heed, and sought out, and set in order many proverbs.'

10. There is a sweet order and wise disposal of the truths set down in Scripture, though we seldom see it by reason of our darkness, and therefore Christ's ministers should digest and put in order the truths they deliver to his people. He first humbles and then comforts; he first gives faith and then holiness, and (which is suitable to the order of doctrine in this book) first weans men's hearts from earthly delights before they can be set upon heavenly ones. For though men do least apprehend a method [orderly arrangement] in Sol-

omon's writings of any other in Scripture, yet here the Spirit of God tells us that there is an order in them: 'He sought out, and set in order many proverbs.'

# 10

# Acceptable words

*Verse 10*

*The preacher sought to find out acceptable words: and that which was written was upright, even words of truth.*

THE second branch of the commendation of the doctrine is taken from the qualities of it, and these are three.

1. First, that what he had studied was 'acceptable words', or as the original bears [signifies], 'words of desire'—that is, purpose worthy of acceptation, fit to gain the desires and delights of men and to take them wholly up [to occupy them completely] in studying to believe and obey them. And this he sets forth as intended by him in all his great diligence.

2. Secondly, what he had written was upright, or as the word signifies, approven [approved] (namely of [by] God), or straight and consonant to [in harmony with] his mind,

and able to make straight (in heart and practice) all that get grace to understand and believe it (see Proverbs 8:8). And this he sets down as the success of his diligent study mentioned in the former branch.

3. Thirdly, that whatever he had affirmed of the vanity of earthly delights, and the worth of holiness in order to a man's happiness, was truth, or firm and worthy to be rested on. In sum, the purpose of this book is fitted powerfully to work upon the affections, being acceptable words, wisely to regulate the practice, being upright or straight words, and solidly to inform the judgment, being words of truth.

Hence learn:

1. Though it is a detestable thing in a minister to study to please the corrupt and sinful humours of men by concealing necessary truths or venting anything contrary to Truth (Galatians 1:10) by extenuating men's sins or speaking peace and comfort to them in their evil ways (Ezekiel 13:18), yet it is very lawful for him to study such a strain and method in delivering Truth, and such a timing of it as may be most pleasing to his hearers for their good to edification (Romans 15:2), and most powerful with them to disengage them from their idols and engage them to Christ and the study of holiness. For this was Solomon's study, worthy to be imitated by all faithful ministers: 'The preacher sought to find out acceptable words.'

2. Although the most part of men loathe the Truth of God, as if it were unworthy to have their spirits and time spent upon it, and they delight more in fables than in most neces-

## Verse 10—Acceptable Words

sary truths (2 Timothy 4:3–4), yet the Truth is of itself worthy of all acceptation. And when the beauty and worth of it is seen in order to the soul's true peace and happiness, it cannot but draw the desires and delights of men (in so far as they are renewed) to embrace and practise it. Therefore the purpose of this book is here called 'acceptable words'.

3. It is not rash, undigested and extemporary discourses that usually are blessed to gain acceptance and to draw toward them the delights and desires of them that are truly wise, but rather such as are digested and accurately sought out by pains in prayer, meditation and other means appointed by God. It must be Satan who suggests prejudices to men's minds against Truth because it is studied and elaborated. For thus Solomon commends the purpose of this book, that he sought 'to find out (which signifies great study) acceptable words'.

4. However many of the truths of God appear unreasonable to unreasonable men (Ezekiel 18:25), such as all unbelievers are (2 Thessalonians 3:2), yet nothing is held forth in Scripture, and nothing can be drawn from it by a right consequence, but what is upright, straight, and consonant to [in agreement with] the mind of God, the rule of all reason and equity. And this being understood and believed, it tends to make men straight in heart and practice (Psalm 119:9), sincere and without dissimulation toward God and man (as the word here translated 'upright' signifies), and directs them in the straight way to their own happiness (2 Timothy 3:17). For, he says, 'That which was written was upright.'

5. Nothing but what is upright, or clearly consonant to the mind of God, should be acceptable to any person. So that before men suffer themselves to be taken with [captivated by] what is held forth as truth, they should try, as the noble Bereans did, whether it is upright or not. For having said he 'sought to find out acceptable words', and speaking of his success as suitable and satisfactory to his desires, he says, 'That which was written was upright.'

6. Where God gives a sincere desire to seek out that which may be for his glory and the edification of others, and to give diligence for that effect, he also blesses the means with some success—though not always in reference to other people's profiting, yet in reference to the instruments' [the preachers'] pains and attaining to the knowledge of his mind. For though Solomon does not say that, having sought to find out acceptable words, he did find words that were acceptable, yet he can say, 'That which was written was upright,' and that was a sufficient reward to him.

7. The Word of the Lord will not deceive or disappoint any that receive it. Those who do not fly from the threatened wrath will find threatenings to be truth and verified upon themselves. And whosoever embraces promises will at last find the accomplishment of them. And, till the Word be looked upon as such, it can never be received or deemed acceptable, as it ought to be. For this is a part of the commendation of it, that it was 'even words of truth'.

# 11

# Wise words

Verse 11

*The word of the wise are as goads, and as nails fastened by the masters of assemblies, which are given from one shepherd.*

IN the third place he commends the Truth from the efficacy and authority of it. And this branch of the commendation he does not apply as before to the purpose contained in this book only, but to the Truth in general, delivered by any whom God sends and qualifies for that end.

1. The expressions seem to be borrowed from shepherds who make use of goads to drive up the dull and sluggish beasts of their flock, and of nails for fixing their folds in which they assemble their flocks, and all this they do at the direction of the chief shepherd or owner of the flock. Under this metaphor is held forth first a twofold effect of the Truth of God:

1) That it is quick and powerful to incite men to their duty and shake off their laziness, which resembles the use of the goad.
2) That it serves to fix, confirm and establish men in the ways of the Lord, and so to prevent their inconstancy, resembled by the use of the nails.

2. Next, there is a description of the dispensers or preachers of this word. They are called the masters of assemblies, or 'collections' as the word is, not as if they had any magisterial or lordly power and authority over the Lord's people assembled, to enjoin anything of their own, but because they preside in public worship and direct the Lord's people how to manage it aright.

3. Thirdly, there is held forth the authority of the Truth, as being given from Christ, as also the authority and subordination of all the preachers of it to him. For these words, 'which are given by one shepherd', may be referred both to the words of the wise which have the aforementioned effects, and to the masters of assemblies, both of these being given from one Shepherd, the Lord Jesus Christ, who was frequently made known to the Church of old by that stile (Ezekiel 34:23 and 37:24; Isaiah 40:11), and who only [alone] has power to make laws and appoint officers in the Church (Isaiah 33:22).

Hence learn:

1. These ministers who do sincerely aim at the edification of the Lord's people and success of his Truth among them will not only commend the Truth as delivered by themselves,

## Verse 11—Wise Words

but they will also commend it as it is delivered by all others who are sent and qualified for that end. It will be their pleasure to see the Truth successful and efficacious in the hands of any faithful minister, and they ought to express this to the people lest, in commending that Truth only which themselves preach, they may seem to be seeking their own esteem and undervaluing others, and so may prejudge [prejudice] the Truth. Therefore Solomon here no less highly commends the Truth delivered by any that are truly wise than he did commend it before as delivered by himself in this book and others of his writing: 'The words of the wise are as goads.'

2. Beside his impotency [complete inability] for what is good, every man naturally has much slowness, backwardness and unwillingness to draw in [take] Christ's yoke, to put forth the power he has in his duty, and to call for that which God is ready to give him. So the Word of the Lord faithfully preached and accompanied with his blessing will give men no ease in their security and neglect of necessary duties, but will be still goading them to these things by serious exhortations and obtestations [earnest supplications]. Though they should spurn against [resist] their teachers if they continue lazy and negligent, it will leave wounds by severe threatenings in their consciences (Acts 2:37). It will divide between the joints and marrow, that they may be forced to fly to Christ the good Samaritan, that he may pour oil in their wounds, and it will cut them sharply (Titus 1:13) by solid refutation of their errors and mistakes. For this efficacy of the Word faithfully preached and accompanied with the powerful blessing of the Chief Shepherd is here set forth under this similitude: 'The words of the wise are as goads.'

3. When people are engaged to Christ, and in some measure established in the Truth and at their duty, they are prone to make defection from it. And therefore the Word serves to fasten them to him, to confirm them in the Truth and in their duty, to unite them among themselves by love, that they may not be henceforth children tossed to and fro with every wind of doctrine, distracted from Christ by their idols, or rent one from another by schisms and divisions. And consequently Christ's ministers should not slightly pass [casually avoid] the pressing of their duty but, by earnest pressing of the Truth and frequent inculcating of their duty by Scripture arguments and motives, should drive it home as a nail in a sure place, that so what they deliver may be as nails fastened.

4. The Lord has appointed that there should be meeting-places for his people to assemble themselves together in, for upholding his visible glory before the world, the mutual upstirring of his people in his service, and that the same Word and ordinance may do good to many at once, from which assemblies none of his people ought to withdraw themselves (Hebrews 10:25). Therefore his public ministers ought to be the principal actors in the worship performed there. They ought to see that these assemblies be frequented, that order and decency be kept in them, that the worship be rightly managed, and all things done in the house of God, according to his own command, in which respects ministers are here called 'the masters of assemblies'.

5. Jesus Christ is the only one (or Chief) Shepherd of the flock, who alone has power to persuade and lead them in the paths of righteousness by the still, running waters (Psalm 23:2–3), who will deal tenderly with the weak lambs and the

## Verse 11—Wise Words

sick of the flock (Isaiah 40:11) and who only has laid down his life for his sheep, for he is here called that 'one shepherd'.

6. Then only the Truth has the aforementioned effects when Christ is the dispenser of it, by the power of his own Spirit conveying it through his sent ministers to his people. And therefore none should take upon them publicly to deliver the Truth but they who are given to the Church from him. Truth should be both delivered and received as that which is given from him. Ministers should beware of delivering anything but what they are sure they have received from him, and people should try both whom and what they hear—for this last clause, 'which are given from one shepherd', may be understood both of the persons and of the words which have the forenamed effects.

# 12

# Profitable study

Verse 12

*And further, by these, my son, be admonished: of making many books there is no end; and much study is a weariness of the flesh.*

THE third article of the conclusion of this book contains an exhortation to the right usemaking [utilising] of the whole, as sufficient to admonish men of their danger and duty, in which all other writings come short. And in pressing this, he doth:

1. First, take up every hearer under that very warm and loving relation of a son, that so he may gain the better acceptance to his message.

2. Next, he shows the principal use to be made of the things he had written—and not of these only, but of all the words of the wise commended in the former verse. That is, of every message of any sent minister of Christ, to wit, that by

VERSE 12—PROFITABLE STUDY

these men should be admonished—the word signifies 'to be enlightened', that is informed—and consequently (according to the sense of our translation) made cautious and wary that they do not make a mistake in so great a matter as this, the discovery of the nearest way to their true happiness.

3. Thirdly, he presses this by two reasons.

1) The first is in these words, 'for in making many books there is no end'. This cannot be understood of the writing of many books like this in hand, to wit books of Scripture, seeing after Solomon's time there behoved to be many books of this sort made—for so he should seem to have condemned the writing of more Scripture, and likewise there is an end put to the making of books of that sort, by closing these books with a curse upon any that should add to them (Revelation 22:18). But the meaning is, that if men do not satisfy themselves with that light and these admonitions which are held out in this book and other Scriptures, they will become vain in their imaginations, and every man will fancy a new and nearer way to happiness than another—and out of his boundless desire of vainglory, will make no end of his enquiry, but will spend the best of his time and strength to vent his own notions and commend his vain imaginations about the way to true happiness, and to confute others (as it is clear natural men of the most refined wits have done in many written volumes). And consequently it is clear he does not condemn the writing or study of other books beside the Scripture (providing they be con-

sonant thereunto [in harmony with Scripture]), but only of such as oppose the Scripture, in so far as they pretend to point out a way to happiness contrary to what is held out therein [in Scripture], by the study of which men's souls can never have true rest or quietness till they close with such truths as are held forth in this book. These truths are as nails fastened by the masters of assemblies, fixing and establishing the hearts of those that receive them, concerning this main query, where their true happiness is to be had.

2) The second reason is that 'much study is a weariness of the flesh'. He speaks of every study opposite to the study of the Truth formerly commended. And the meaning is that he who will apply himself to any other study for attaining to true happiness may well weary his flesh: he shall do no more good to himself, he shall bring no true profit or satisfaction to his soul, and therefore it is the part of every child of wisdom to apply himself to the making use of these truths formerly commended.

Hence learn:

1. When ministers have held forth light and given warning to people concerning their duty and danger, they must be very earnest with them to admit and make use of that, and must not think themselves sufficiently exonerated to have held forth light and given warning to people unless they do their utmost to prevail with them to make use of it. For so Solomon does here: after clear light held forth concerning men's duty and warning given of their hazard in case they

## VERSE 12—PROFITABLE STUDY

neglect it, he is most serious with them to make use of his pains. 'Further, by these, my son, be admonished' (or enlightened).

2. This is the perfection of Scripture above all other writings in the world, that every part of it which has been delivered to the Church by any penman contains a perfect rule of faith and manners, so that no other writings beside or contrary to it are necessary for supplying the defects of it. For Solomon here supposes that what he and others of the Lord's servants who lived before and in his time had written (though then there was but a small part of Holy Scripture delivered to the Church) was sufficient to admonish men of their duty and hazard in order to their true happiness, while he says by these, 'My son, be admonished.'

3. In the study of the Scripture, men should not aim at their comfort only, but mainly that they may receive clear information and warning of their sin and hazard, the true remedy of it, and the way to attain to it. For this is one main use to be made of this book, and consequently of the rest of Scripture: 'By these be admonished.'

4. Though some of the hearers of the gospel be strong men in comparison of others who are but babes (1 John 2:13–14), yet all of them should come as children to hear the Lord's mind with meekness and submission to the reproofs and warnings of the Word, with love to their teachers, desiring the sincere milk of the Word from them. And ministers should put on bowels of fatherly affection toward the people with whom they deal. Therefore Solomon here speaks to every hearer as a son: 'By these, my son, be admonished.'

5. Men are naturally so transported [overwhelmed] with a desire of vainglory, especially that which they affect to have by their wisdom (Job 11:12), that while they have time or strength, they will never make an end of seeking out many inventions by which to attain to their imaginary happiness: after they have written one book to show themselves wise in the discovery of the way to happiness, they will still begin another. And yet, so empty are all the creatures and courses that natural men can take about them that, till men betake themselves to that new and living way to happiness which the Scripture reveals, they will meet with nothing but endless labour and continual disappointment, without any true settling or quietness to their minds. For Solomon speaking of their writings (people who mistake the Scriptures' way to happiness) says, 'Of making many books there is no end.'

6. The study of saving knowledge may prove wearisome to the flesh, partly by reason of our dullness and unacquaintance with the grounds of consolation and confidence of success, and partly because the Lord will have the wearying of the flesh in that study a mean to promove mortification [a way to promote self-denial] and to divert the heart from sinful delights. Though that is so, yet that study is sweet of itself, and is the very rest and refreshment of the soul—yea it is health to the spirit and marrow to the bones, and in comparison of it, all other studies are spending and wearisome even to the flesh. For this study must be rest and sweetness, seeing it is of other studies only that Solomon affirms this: 'Much study is a weariness of the flesh.'

# 13

# Fear God

Verse 13

*Let us hear the conclusion of the whole matter: Fear God, and keep his commandments: for this is the whole duty of man.*

HERE is the last article of the conclusion of this book, containing the sum of Solomon's scope in the whole, especially in these directions which he had given for attaining to true happiness.

1. And this sum he first presses upon his own heart and the hearts of all others, and so labours to fasten it as a nail there, and as that which the whole purpose of this book aims at.

2. Secondly, he branches out this sum in two exhortations.
   1) The first is an exhortation to the fear of God. Sometimes in Scripture that is put for the whole worship and service of God (Isaiah 29:13). But being here distinguished from the keeping of the command-

ments, which comprehends all the worship of God, it is to be understood of that inward filial reverence and awe of God which the Lord has promised in the covenant of grace to put in the hearts of his people. By it, out of a believing consideration of the greatness and sovereignty of God (Jeremiah 10:6–7) and his goodness to them in Christ (Hosea 3:5)—especially his proneness to pardon their failings (Psalm 130:4)—they do depart from what they know is offensive to their Father (Proverbs 16:6) and aim at what is well-pleasing in his sight (Philippians 2:12), in humble confidence making use of Christ's merits to cover their imperfections and make them acceptable to God (Psalm 5:7).

2) The second exhortation is to the keeping of his commandments. By this is not meant a legal perfect obedience, which Solomon knew to be impossible, he being so well acquainted with original corruption (Ecclesiastes 7:20, 29), but a sincere and constant aim at conformity to the will of God, without exception of any of his commands, and that because they are his.

3. And thirdly, he presses this study by two arguments. The first is, in this verse, that 'this is the whole duty of man' or, as the words are in the original, 'this is the whole of man', to wit his main task or a compend [summary] of all that God requires and works in his own, and by which they should be wholly taken up all their lifetime, as they desire to be truly happy here and hereafter.

## Verse 13—Fear God

Hence learn:

1. It is necessary for Christ's ministers that they have some certain scope relating to the practice of the Lord's people, at which they should aim in all that they deliver to them. And in the close of any discourse or part of their pains, they should labour to leave some impression of it as a nail fastened in their hearts. For so Solomon here sums up his scope in this book and labours to fix the same in the hearts of all men: 'Let us hear the conclusion of the whole matter.'

2. Whatever duty ministers press upon people in order to their peace and happiness, they should imprint the same upon their own hearts and become learners of these lessons they hold out to others, not binding heavy burdens upon men's backs, which they touch not with one of their fingers. For Solomon here makes himself a hearer and learner of his own doctrine, while he says, 'Let us hear the conclusion of the whole matter: fear God, and keep his commandments: for this is the whole duty of man.'

3. No man will ever be such a proficient [an expert] in the study of the fear and obedience of the Lord as that he will not need to learn more and to advance in that study. For Solomon was now near the close of his days, and at a good degree of perfection in that study, and yet he incites himself and those who are furthest advanced to greater progress in this: 'Fear God, and keep his commandments.'

4. They that would see good days and live in the light of the Lord's countenance must learn to be in his fear all the day long, entertaining the faith of his greatness and goodness,

that so they may be kept from these things which impede their fellowship with him, in which their felicity consists. For, while he sums up his directions for attaining to true happiness, which he had proved impossible to be found in earthly things, and only to be had in fellowship with God reconciled in Christ, he gives this for one principal part of that sum: 'Fear God.'

5. Man's true happiness is only to be found in keeping the commands of God. He cannot expect a sweet meeting with God (Isaiah 64:5) or the comfortable manifestations of his love (John 14:21, 23) but in that way, for this is the other part of the sum of his directions for attaining to true happiness which consists in communion with God: 'Keep his commandments.'

6. The fear of the Lord is the root and principle of all right obedience to him, without which men cannot act or move acceptably in any commanded duty. Therefore he presses the study of the fear of God in order to acceptable obedience: 'Fear God, and keep his commandments.'

7. Where the fear of God is in the heart, there will be also a care of keeping his commands manifested in the practice, and that fear will evidence itself by some endeavour after a suitable walking to his commands. For the keeping of the commandments here pressed may be looked on as the evidence and fruit of the fear of God: 'Fear God, and keep his commandments.'

8. However men that seek their happiness in this earth look upon the study of the fear and obedience of the Lord as no

## Verse 13—Fear God

part of their business in order to the attaining of their fancied happiness, but rather an impediment in the way to it (Malachi 3:14), yet this same blessed study is the great end for which man was made—the only study that is worthy to have his spirit wholly exercised about it, so as all his other studies ought to be subordinated to this. And the consideration of this should be a strong motive to put him to it, as is imported in this reason: 'For this is the whole duty of man.'

# 14

# The Final Judgment

### Verse 14

*For God shall bring every work into judgment, with every secret thing, whether it be good, or whether it be evil.*

THE last reason by which he presses this blessed study of living in the fear and obedience of the Lord is taken from the certainty and exactness of the Last Judgment.

At that time, both men's more open and visible actions and their more secret plots and closest contrivances (of what sort soever, whether good or bad) shall be brought forth to receive sentence, reward or punishment according to their nature. And therefore they that desire to be truly happy here and hereafter would [ought to] leave off the pursuit of earthly vanities and sinful delights and apply themselves to this study: to 'fear God and keep his commandments, which is the whole duty of man'.

## Verse 14—The Final Judgment

Hence learn:

1. The best of God's children may have their hearts sometimes so hardened and so averse from his fear and the duties of new obedience that they need to have that dreadful day of judgment represented to them (as one of the goads formerly mentioned) to keep their hearts in awe and to excite them to their duty. For this reason is held out as useful to be considered by all that desire to be truly happy, and as that by which Solomon pressed upon his own heart, the study of living in the fear and obedience of the Lord: 'For God shall bring every work into judgment, with every secret thing, whether it be good, or whether it be evil.'

2. So exact will the Last Judgment be, that no action or purpose of men shall escape the cognisance and sentence of the Judge in that day. Their public sins shall then be published to all, and their secret sins shall then be laid open, even these of their hearts, which they have got altogether hid [hidden] from the eyes of the world, and which they studied along their life to hide them from their own consciences by neglecting to search them out and mourn for them. The consideration of this should deter men from secret sins. 'For', he says, 'God will bring every work into judgment, with every secret thing.'

3. The best actions of the godly considered in themselves cannot abide the trial of God's judgment (Psalm 143:2) by reason of the sinful mixture which is in them (Isaiah 64:6). And so they shall not come into judgment or condemnation (Romans 8:1). Yet as they are perfumed with Christ's merits and made perfect by him in whom believers are complete

(Colossians 2:10), they shall be brought forth to judgment to receive the reward of grace which the righteous Judge shall give in that day. 'For', he says, 'every work shall come into judgment, whether it be good or evil.'

4. All the evil actions of men—which they now refuse to look upon, that they might mourn and make use of the blood of Christ for cleansing of them—shall in that great day be set in the light of their countenance and made patent for their shame and terror before men and angels, that they may receive for them deserved wrath to the utmost. This should be considered by men when they are tempted to sin, and by secure impenitent slighters [disparagers] of their former wickedness. For 'God will bring every work into judgment, whether it be good, or whether it be evil'.

5. That last solemn action of the Last Judgment, which will be in a manner between time and eternity, deserves men's most frequent and serious consideration. Without this, men will never get their hearts alienated from pursuing perishing vanities and sinful delights as their chief good, nor engaged to the study of true piety. For as both the Old and New Testament close with representing to men's thoughts the Last Judgment and many particular books of Scripture, so this divine preacher closes his book with it, as that which should be much in the thoughts of the Lord's people, who should live so as they may daily desire to see this day 'when God will bring every work into judgment, with every secret thing, whether it be good, or whether it be evil'.

Even so, come, Lord Jesus.